The Currency

The Currency

Paul Otremba

Four Way Books
Tribeca

Editorial Office
Four Way Books
POB 535, Village Station
New York, NY 10014
www.fourwaybooks.com

Library of Congress Cataloging-in-Publication Data

Otremba, Paul.
The currency / Paul Otremba.
p. cm. -- (A Stahlecker series selection)
ISBN 978-1-884800-89-4 (pbk. : alk. paper)
I. Title.
PS3615.T74C87 2009
811'.6--dc22

2008043331

This book is manufactured in the United States of America and printed on acid-free paper.

Four Way Books is a not-for-profit literary press. We are grateful for the assistance we receive from individual donors, public arts agencies, and private foundations.

This publication is made possible with public funds from the National Endowment for the Arts and from the New York State Council on the Arts, a state agency.

NATIONAL ENDOWMENT FOR THE ARTS

State of the Arts NYSCA

Distributed by University Press of New England
One Court Street, Lebanon, NH 03766

[clmp]
We are a proud member of the Council of Literary Magazines and Presses.

TABLE OF CONTENTS

Part III

For my family

I

Novecento

is a horse hung from the ceiling, the dumb
hoisted weight and the weight of the harness,

the already anachronistic machinery of it.
We walk around in circles, thinking history.

The legs are too long, acute impressions
the extension's been severed: dried up

taproots, brainstems held in solution.
The solution is to hoist it. That's what

the machine's for. History's coarse hair,
a skin stretched over re-collected bones.

We walk around in circles, imagining a room
above this one, where the horse is carried

off to, imagining the many uses for the meat
that must have piled on the taxidermist's floor.

Gray Windows

Against gray's generation of gray, the city's
empty face, the clouds crack enough to give
a sudden shock of yellow, the taxi reflecting
my something of need, inarticulate, then here,
the burst of twenty suns in just as many
windows, the point I enter, the calls' quick
punctures, suturing the song, the dozen or so
birds who decide spontaneously to make
this tree tonight's frenzied hotspot. Not here,
then suddenly so aware of *bird*, of *riot*,
the light, a thick gloss on magnolia leaves,
another surface for me to claim myself by.

Not a painting, but *I have made a place*,
Rothko said of his windows, the red
rectangles on red I brooded into or out of,
allowed only the ridges of brushstroke
and my mood, what I had brought to it,
mixed with the sheer intensity of color
and size of the canvas, big enough
to cover my apartment floor, indulgent
as my thoughts: church window, church
graveyard, or a portrait, the figure a Medici,
behind whose head the open window told
how the bird got in, that the soul had left.

The wind clicked the saw grass, a clatter
of bones. I knew the red flash from the cypress
as a cardinal, lighting out beyond the house,
the canal. What makes a space inhabitable?
The day before, on a trip to Charleston,
we were forced across the dead, their stones
creating a path through the churchyard,
so we couldn't forget it wasn't about them.
On the bank of the canal, thick with mud,
with grass, the canal itself the only monument
for the slaves who built it, I watched crabs
sparring over holes the ebb tide abandoned.

In my half-sleep I heard the sharp voices
surrounding my bed slowly pulled back
to where they'd come from, the bars emptying
down the street and an argument breaking out
beneath my window. Knowing I was safe
was like knowing the self as the heart felt
inside the ear, the body as its many rooms:
attic crawlspaces of the mind, a root cellar
for fear. There are nights I wake to a room
I don't understand at first as my own,
until the light through the blinds separates
what it touches, a blue weight from blue dark.

Between where I sit and the branches' reach
is a thin pane of glass, my reflection a film
kept out and in, drinking coffee, given
the privacy of a tree, the intimacy of a cup,
which is only a cup because it holds,
while the ringed stains of coffee inscribe
a private language. How can I know
the eye without its names? The city
except as diorama? I look outside and see
tree, see *bird*: the wax sheen of magnolia
leaves colonizing red brick, the greased
arrowheads of starlings, low across the stage.

This Wren

For no reason at all this wren, this little mound
of pencil shavings. But what appears is too bleared,

too gray sluice of clouds covering the window
so the kitchen goes dim. So this wren eating beneath

scratches of juniper, of field grass, little mounds
of graphite in the beak. For no reason I let

the sauce simmer, the reduction gone syrup.
Then she enters, asking about the drawing, a turkey,

five fingers dragging a wind through the grass,
and the wren goes on with the little mounds of seed.

More questions arise about the timing, the meat of it,
the delicacy of a still, cold center. For no reason at all,

rosemary, *Money Jungle*, track "Fleurette Africaine,"
and the wren finds a hole in the rosebush,

while she places heavy plates in orbit around the table,
singing a wordless "Fleurette Africaine," a little wren,

a little monster, sweet door in the rosebush.
For no reason at all a monster in the wren's nest.

Conservatory

I saw it once, the place full of steam,
from behind the taxi's streaked window.

But in the park we were vulnerable,
exposed for the sky's opening. Running,

a small space opened near the small
of her back. Some nights I would

wake there. Then in dreams, her tongue
reflected with scales like the sides

of a glass fish. And there were other—
more important—rains. Still, what leaves?

What conservation of mettle? More dreams
proceeded, but the order came out wrong.

It was a vastness, the glass against the sky,
another couple up for anything,

or so it seemed from the railing.
On the sides of the glass fish swam

scrutiny, an abundance of fern.
And still others came by and said, Oh,

not that red, *that* red.

Weaving

> *I don't think they'll find the new weaving*
> *anywhere finer than truth.*
>
> —Osip Mandelstam

I've tried to sift a truth finer than salt
from my mouth. It matters: I get up

or I do not. The books can wait, leaves
burn themselves these days, and the day

begins or it does not. Now wingless,
a wasp masquerading as the sun crawls—

a harmless razor—across the backlit
curtain. No city trembles on the verge

of the sea. No stupid bird threatens
to dissolve me if I forget my species

in the official questionnaire. I could
put my ten bureaucrats to their task.

The dusting and polishing. There's a point,
a mirror for me to enumerate my teeth.

Beyond these walls, there's only the snowed-in
field, an egg just opened but empty.

Offices

Florence, 2005

His face darkened by accrual of oil and dirt, he was asking
for "some money," some change we didn't have,
which was hard to explain, which made us no less
cursed, no less the "fucking-shit-people."
                                        In the square,
a few young men, Africans (lacking permits), quickly
folded their displays, sunglasses and handbags,
then dispersed into the crowd, eyes straining back
around corners.
                An expression I'd find on Artemisia's
Holofernes: the stalk half shorn, half-shriek
off a face surprised the meat gives in so easily.
Judith all business-like, like evidence.
                                        For the 17th century
what's shocking isn't the measuring by stretches and tears—
violation given a circumference—but the brutality
of her trial having been so public.
                                    The matter settled,
Orazio Gentileschi welcomed Agostino back
into the household, perhaps placing his hands on his friend's
shoulders. Perhaps kissed his cheeks.
                                        What virtue asks
of the head is that it comes off only, not cleanly.
                                                Is something
wrong with me that I can't hold to a violence requiring
another one? Lacking *telos*. We were, after all,
the "fucking-shit-people."
                            With rivulets in the bedsheets,
what I should look for is blood's realism—

what I read somewhere.
                                                This story was told to me
by a young university student: there was a diplomat
in Rome, who didn't believe (that part's questionable)
the Bernini statue was really marble, the depression
of the thigh where Pluto's hand grasps, that stone
could do that, so they made an exception, and he was
allowed to touch it.
                                          In the crowd, the two plainclothes
detectives were recognizably detectives.
                                                                  Meat giving in
so easily beneath, not virginal white, but Artemisian
gold—
          One doesn't need to enjoy the thing, only mean it.

Childhood Monochrome

I parade around in a skin until I own it. My eyes' blue
keeps what I find. All else becomes a curtain of blue.

Mother's apron, sheep's wool, "Bah-Bah": my mouth's
my best idea. My idea tugs at her apron strings, their blue.

Blue, the portrait of my mother in the kitchen, is a child's
scrawl, a room which cannot remain except for blue.

Who is not in the room dies suddenly when I see her,
dishes drying in the sink, the window open and blue.

The pattern on the table is German (or Dutch?), a gift
from my grandmother: leaves of white lined by blue.

My face in the bathwater looks up at you. Round
moon, Mother, on the world's surface, stained by blue.

Now I lay me down… to a place in the mind. *And if I die…*
God's idea, before I wake, a bruise retaining its blue.

Who's not in the room watching, blind as the saint
I'm named for, waits in a darkness torn from blue.

Exit

This is a desert country, and we are passing
        through it. Patches of tamped, dry grasses,

patches of brush in the falling-back, fall
        away outside the window. With night

coming on, truck-lights bulge and blear.
        Like we are waking. Like we have

been here before, or always, counting
        trucks pass (in threes), watching white

lines puncture—extend—ticking off:
        gash, suture, cicatrix. They merge

now slick as whales, now low hills
        banked against the bleached-bone-

arc of sky, where for disruption—pixilated
        in and out of focus—lights slur,

slack round Os of mouths, and freeze.
        Grief, then, the look of it. Three trucks, one

tilting. Three rectangles. What the eyes
        enter, would catch, is "YELLOW,"

immovable, is sere, ice, sand, glass.
	This is a desert country. *We could turn off here,*

you say, *find jobs.* People do that sort of thing.
	What was it to wake here? To find

the tortoise shell: cars stacked on cars
	for hauling? Nobody turns off—

the sky in mirror acts out the sky,
	the film on which light sticks is expanded.

The lone tower's lit; your face
	shadowed with rain, with insects. The sky

in its bruise is split. Dark flowering,
	beckon. Red signal above dry grasses,

flash here, now here, a necklace.

Gorgias in Love

To say we have a history means she was sitting on the bed.
Having length, breadth, and depth. In the movie, the man
who's lost his short-term memory writes his lover's name

in reverse across his chest. But without two known points,
a thing remains boundless. Neither unmappable, nor veered
off, nor a gap. It's best to think of it as a problem, like if

the ground is wet, it is raining. A November or March,
in the hallway or bedroom, either we were in love
or not. For example, *If you walk out*—I wish to discuss

the nature of things. The bedroom with nightstand
and alarm clock and a nightstand and alarm clock.
In the movie, we do unspeakable things to one another.

The lover finds out to love means outside of time,
while remaining aware it could end any moment.
Knowing the distance from mirror to light switch

we can find the bed. The name spelled out, rightly,
in the reflection. Do we hang the mirror on this wall
or this wall? Her on the bed or near the window.

Hearing the name repeated isn't the same as tasting it.
Slightly embarrassed, contemptuous, but even so,
pleasant. To the ultimatum, walking out the door.

Yet if the gap's irreducible, then what to make of failure?
For example, a man flying over the sea. Let's
assume falling. The apartment window faces the light

of late-night Chinese take-out and a three-story magnolia tree.
What burns to illuminate and what must be filled in later.
The man who can't remember writes above his bed

(in French), the one I love is the one sleeping *next to me.*
A pipeline from bed to door, by which the words get sent,
the consequence's clear. We behave badly. Or,

near me. How to say that? The lover marks her thighs
with arrows, and the man forgets to count the stops
made by the train. She carefully constructs her words

and attaches to them a name. But necessary and named
doesn't make a thing desirable. At this moment, a man is flying
over the sea, so we need a new test case. To each their beetle

and their beetle-box. The homonymic clamor, a hail
like "gorgeous." It's what I'd call amber, but a shade or two
darker, opaque, and thumb-shaped, asleep or only bored.

What gets filled in later. In the movie, there is a difference
between forgetting the one who sleeps next to you
and forgetting to bring change for the parking ramp. But

how to say that? Outside the apartment, the sky was either
snow or rain. Let's assume we were in love or not in love.
The beetle crosses the floor in this direction, then this direction.

Everyone Remembers Icarus

It caught us by surprise, a late wave
of frost breaking blossom-heavy
limbs, and our steps thinned
a few wings from the trees. What rose
was a dampness, a waxy taste
in the throat. It all felt so derivative:
wet cherry blossoms *looking* like
cherry blossoms. The way the Capitol,
set back behind graffitied barriers,
seemed a tourist's photograph
of the thing and still not the thing
we wanted. But when were we not

accumulating the endless
evidence against ourselves?
Because he was old, the poet
was having trouble reading
his own words, even magnified:
a single finger stumbled across the page.
Then leaving, you recalled a certain line
to me, how we, too, had done things
badly and could hold flight
above failure. Yes, the boy flew,
but he still remains foolish.
I take back nothing. I regret nothing.

II

ABSTRACT

When I'm finally ready to start
believing in something else,
a landscape, say, completely

annihilated by snow, I move
to where the view of the rocks
becomes clearer, the angular

gray gaps caught in the smear
of blankness, with its ridged,
fuzzy texture of a whiteout.

Or it's a line drawn over
a period of years, across
a series of canvases, which never

is the same, only bolder
or erased, separating the various
thicknesses and densities, how

that year must have passed
quietly for him, at least no one
he knew managed to get

their heart pummeled, but this
one was spent with his face
pressed to a corner, licking

at some inarticulate wound,
with a wish to be narrow,
almost invisible, but insisting,

Look at me. Or it's the glacial
slide of blue into a shade
of blue just darker, the tension

of that pose, and the immense
effort it must have taken
not to give the day its story.

The Currency

That summer, the twenty-first century
was reams of plastic around thick metal
rings, forming a woman on her back,
stretching forty feet beneath the river's
surface. Three times a day, tourists
gathered to take pictures at the bridge,
a flock of clicks capturing the magmatic
gurgle and slow rise of the water
goddess, Our Lady of Prague,
what the artist saw as a birth into
the new century, yet sprung up whole
like wisdom, a stirring in the thigh,
and she had synthesizers on the bank,
playing a music we might predict
for some silver-clad future. Glitter
was what that country had foreseen
for itself, payment in full for relentless
occupations. For the young, this was
their kingdom come: couples kissing
in the subway and on escalators.
The old men, too, weren't afraid
to be seen eating ice cream, slouching
in well-worn work suits—lime green?
Grass green? A color striking enough,
yet devoid of distinction, it still served
to cover the people's street sweepers.

Fumbling at the counter with a few
well-worn phrases, you and I were

involved in all that—buying pastries
we couldn't pronounce but only
pointed to, our money going further than
we'd eat—and yet alien when our lips
touched, lacking any "philosophical
significance," just hunger, loneliness,
what I felt each time I took the bridge
coming home, passing the vendors,
the statue worn out by touch: Saint
John of Nepomuk, patron of crossing
over, faithful council, deadman's float.
Even when we knew I'd be leaving
soon, I stopped to listen to the girl
selling her clay pipes: a small grace
so amazed it had currency at all.

The Birds

I. Tether

I saw it fast, the small
thing wounded, and smaller
for seeming so willingly
breakable and displaced,
the handful of feathers being
lifted off the train's platform,
then falling back, as if the bird
were trying to fly against
an invisible string playing
with it, pulling it down

to the tiles. Sprawled
on the steps, leaning on elbows,
the boy watched (and could
watch) the bird struggle, his
face—unmoved—unmovable,
or so I thought, until I saw
what he saw, not one bird
but two, and the unguarded
white where the claws curled—
opened against.

II. Slide

What looked, at first,
like wet wool, a child's lost
hat unthawed from the snow,

suddenly stared back
from a small mangled eye,
the bird's feathers mashed

to a slick of dark matter
around the gape, in what
was once the stomach,

exposing the light rigging
of bones, some recognizable
intention that disrupted the fine

shale beneath my thinking,
and the larger, more
unsupportable blocks

finally gave way
as in the dream I had where
my younger brother died,

and I couldn't believe
in a world that would not
have him. His face composed

out of faces on the street,
then a picture on a lamppost,
a reflection's vicissitude

in a storefront window—him,
not him—he was everywhere
never long enough,

and I needed a way to account
for this—
so a god, an afterlife.

III. ***The Birds***

Then for each length of wire stretched between two poles,
one dark bird, and Missouri falling back behind them,
while the sun—another harbinger—fell, too, collecting
in the runoff pools, its orange light skimmed, my eye

snagging against surfaces.

In the Hitchcock, what we don't see are the thin strings
of nylon looped around the legs, so the birds couldn't fly
away, but formed the odd, live kites tethered to the actress.
When she moved, they moved. So even if she were innocent,

they'd still come.

Coverage

This is live. The head hangs, as the face—

not really panicked, but not just excited—appears
off, expanded, like we are watching him

underwater, so tethered there, anchored, and the news

he has is happening. At this moment, fire's distortion
lights the screen, eerily yellow in an eerily green sky,

like the city's fallen, been swept off to sea.

But it's a desert, and I know this as I make the sound

vanish, like it remains inside an aquarium. The room's
filled with green light, and I start to get ready

for the concert, a birthday, a promise I made

to take my brother to hear Handel. This is happening.
The landscape flares (then vanishes), with the mouth

mouthing mutely.

Messiah

To accommodate the distance between cities,
the topography's changed

...make straight
in the desert a highway.

I take the exit through
a community's erasure, up the cathedral's hill
to the higher ground of the city
...her warfare
is accomplish'd.

What I don't see happens
quickly, the shape not there, then the man already
in the road, a few feet from where my car stops.

Not fear, but his eyes set cold, like he's been
outside all night, like his clothes and face
suggest, then erupting,

his hands pounding
the hood of the car, against those who won't
see him, to

...break them with a rod of iron;
...dash them in pieces like a potter's vessel.

Rest Stop

We stopped so she could ease out
the tension building in her calf muscle,
a knot from being cramped together
too long in the car. Our anger had become

just another thing we couldn't commit to,
and taken up by the heat, it joined
the sticky calm stretched between us.
Near where we parked, a young woman

rested a bottle against her neck,
the water mixing with sweat, and she pulled
her short hair into slick, limp peaks;
while probing their car's overheated engine,

the serpentine, tattooed arms of her boyfriend,
or husband, moved out and in. Her look said
they could have been going from Oklahoma
to "kiss my ass," passing the restaurant chains

and strip malls, but caught there in the parking lot,
a distraction for families vacationing.
When we heard their voices becoming clearly
a name, we knew it was a mother

and father calling, what we all fear.
These were the kind of people who could lose
a child: frantic, almost chiding the boy,
who must only be playing a child's trick.

Behind a tree, he became the tree, and his face
contained all faces of children emptying
from sedans. In no time, in a time that now seems
impossible, a crowd had gathered for the search,

and when I looked from the mother to the woman
I was with, what looked back was inconsolable.
Trickster, not the boy but the angel,
don't come to make good on your promise,

your dark reprimand. There was no angel.
And the boy was found down by the dog park.
Over the small, round rise of her stomach,
he rested his arm, the inked coils of a snake.

Vigil

What was it, then, that was asked of me,
while the room folded in, and they stood
hovering, their faces unmade, darkening?

And beyond those shadows waited other
shadows, so much to refute. My throat
opened like a throat stretched bare,

expectant and vulnerable, to echo
their voices appeasing me, what I only
half heard, even after waking to my fever

passed, light entering the window bruised,
and my parents retreating from the door:
what I've been trying to conjure tonight

as I've watched you shift in your uneasy
sleep, those words they'd used to calm
the heat I carried so close beneath skin.

The Room

We woke to it still here: a room
for dressing quietly, another lit
by the TV's glare. In the scene,
we were performing the scene

where we are hung in the silences
we'd finally crush between fingers,
so what started out as anger
could exit by way of its own juices.

To get it while it was hot, her first,
then the words I said, the not-me
words went straight for the throat,
the ego's thin root, before I

retreated behind a cheap-shot
stare: *Don't think of coming near.*
If only the core were more malleable,
it might fit through the teeth,

if there was a core. I'd explain this
better, how what maneuvered behind
the face felt inside as inside,
the eye's insect pressed to the screen,

how the room seemed to lean
into its own *roomness.* The shape
defined there was something I could
break against: her, my identical,

inextricably other, reflecting image
fractured, the web splaying through glass.

Cleaning-House

Strung out beside us, and not
        shadows, the still rising, still
    gathering lights shot beneath

the surface, but not breaking
        the water and widening shape
    of my reflection in the white

wake. With a good catch,
        we'd have pike, four or five
    chained through the gills

along the boat, packed in
        the water to keep them fresh,
    until my father could clean them,

which was the knife, its clouded
        tongue opening the length
    of their narrow bellies. I was

supposed to be watching. I saw
    the glint of skin. The plastic container.

—⁓—

They return to the lake,
        as they've done every summer
    since her childhood. In the morning

father and daughter untie from
                    the dock, head out for the dark
          places sunk beneath reeds,

fallen trees where the bass hide.
                    It's noon on the first day, and still
          they've caught nothing, when

she feels the slight tension,
                    watches her line slice water.
          Just like he's taught her,

she holds the blackened-green
                    body of the fish to the boat's floor,
          then her final act of kindness,

to quicken its release, she lets
          the small hammer fall against it—

—~—

when she tells me this, she looks
                    hard, to see if I'll believe her,
          the hammer, the kindness.

When it didn't die, she struck
                    again, only making things
          worse, which continued until

her father stepped in, and they
headed back to shore. It wasn't
until later at the diner, when

he reached across the table
for the check, that she couldn't
decide if the feeling rising

in her was a form of helplessness
or hate, as when my father
handed me the knife (my eye

floating dimly in the stains),
I tried to find the one clean cut.

Noise Like Wings

Pressed between hands and what I made of them,
then smoothed against the café's clean window,
the page clung to traces of numerous refoldings
and the grime-incised fingers of the man
holding it, pointing to a few adhered photographs
for his friend, equally caked with the street
they must sleep in, both of them unaware—
or tired of caring—we were watching them,
but from inside the window, reminding you
of a play, of *all the dead voices,* their *noise*

like wings. Like leaves. The sun lit the pictures
to sudden shapes gathering, figures etched
in a thick translucency, but reversed, shadowy,
and through the veil of paper, thin glare
of window, I couldn't know who'd entered them,
or if the photographs were even his. It mattered
to me, as if the visibly enfolding bodies
could have explained the misshapen letters
he'd scrawled in between the frames,
whether they contained story or were only

a corrupt mind's ciphers, empty vessels,
like all the discarded bottles we later found
frozen in the canal. A story's what I'm trying
to build myself now that you've returned
to that other coast you never stopped calling
home, a story where I tell you how the peonies

flashed here, are now implosions, pulped
like so much soaked paper, how in this
morning's light, I almost heard them move,
the figures beneath the photographs' gloss.

III

Event Horizon

I.

Tree limbs frosted, coral-like,
and the air a sea drained between bluffs

above the river, and cold like I imagine
the sea at its submerged horizon,

a green light going gray, then a gray
too impassable, or here, ice buckling

at a bend in the river, where the eye
reaches over, falling on the far shore.

The cold cracks ice, a branch
somewhere breaking, and beneath me,

along the bank, a younger version
of myself released bottles against

the sandstone to hear the sharp crashing
ring, out of boredom, or parading

my frustration with the universe,
the injustice of being young (and therefore

frustrated), for the collapsing parabolas
of assembled swallows, feeding off

the sudden flood of insects,
while the last light stopped at the leaves.

II.

Another river, another cold
landscape crumpled above and within

the water. This second river, grown
thick and sluggish, piled up against

the bend, where seeing naturally
emptied into the event, the far shore.

It was a sound I'd come to anticipate,
the dull dropping of snow from trees,

and not the far-off explosions,
streaking the camera's panoramic night-

vision and a sky, filtered green, caught
rippling, aquatic, above a city's shaded

spires, each building and hill
made low, bleached by the bursts

glowing hot as phosphorus, white
as salt. Not real, and yet not un-

real: the city under siege (like *Love*
or *Clouds*, things Keats said *require*

a greeting of the Spirit to make them
wholly—which is to say, meaningful—

exist, transfigured, since the city
would have burned (and did burn) without me).

The Physician

I. Self-Portrait: The Physician's Son

My father made me watch as he stitched
my finger, "Aren't you curious?" Quiet
kitchen, waitresses arriving, you liked
that part, steadied the leek. The knife

only did what it was meant to, a good
knife, but one hand turned on its brother.
In some interpretations, it was a tool,
not murder, in the beginning. Stove hot.

Cat soft. Nipple hungry. Mine. His mother
in the next room, the child practiced
his hammers. *Such a good boy*, always
serving the mouth. *This is the church,*

this is the steeple, open it up… Hands
between legs at night, maybe. Maybe
not. Was it her hand on my stomach
that excited me? Or the thought of what

came next? Thief, in another time
you would have paid for this, been
severed from the root. "You're not
watching," my father said, then,

“not another stitch until…” until
I looked. I couldn’t even feel my finger,
not my finger. Clipping the thread’s
edges, he left the smallest scar.

II. The Physician at Wentworth Place

The accrual on the tongue,
metallic, over-brimming,
and more than blood, *arterial,*
I know it. I've nursed it.

Metallic, over-brimming,
my throat fills with a boiling sea,
unknowable, but nursed
to a fleck conspiring on the sheet.

A throat full of a boiling sea,
not the closed-fisted poppy.
The fleck conspiring on the sheet
untangles chest, rope of brain.

And not the closed fists of poppies,
wine-dark, purple-mouthed,
but hands inside the rope of brain,
imagination's true color of blood—

wine-dark, purple-mouthed,
the rich accrual on the tongue.
I know the colour of that blood:
more than blood: *arterial.*

III. ***Self-Portrait with Dr. Arrieta***

The body, by its look
not so much flesh
as an oily residuum, the meat
puttied and rank with what ails it, is cradled
by the doctor. In Goya's self-portrait

let's say this doctor is not like
the three faces forming, or un-
forming, out of reason's inchoate
smear in the background,
the monsters let loose by some failing,

the painter still could not hear him,
being deaf.
                    But in the vortex of the voices'
incantation, at the "Country House
of the Deaf Man," the artist's hand-me-down
asylum outside Madrid,

the eye dug Goya in further.
Like Saturn to his children,
he watched what his own hands did.
He must have known a world still
existed beyond him, so he placed Arrieta,

his savior, into this self-portrait,
between his own body and the dark
figures emulsified in their stain,
these shadowy sisters:
sickness, madness, and obscurity.

The doctor holds up Goya's body
to help him catch a drink from the glass,
the sturdy elixir, as light pours in from
the unknown source, touching their faces.
He knows what the doctor's holding.

He's painted himself with his eyes shut.

Haute Cuisine

The pig couldn't know it was a pig,
not because it lacked a conspicuous
preference for truffles over the few
rotten turnips set aside for the trash,

but because when I looked, there was
a thin slit of a smile across its throat,
which explained the pig's patience
with the cooks. One punched holes

his friend filled with garlic, each twist
of the blade loosening the meat
from a word rising in my own throat,
as I scoured dishes in the sink,

an orange slither of oil inscribed
on the surface. But the pig couldn't
know it was a pig. No hooves
hammered against steel counters,

there was no last leap onto the stove.
The cooks, too, had only a slim
notion: one sang along with the radio,
the other wiped his hands on his shirt.

Redwing Blackbird

Before the floor
gave out—his father's

speech taken—where
they would walk,

the path a clipped
moon arcing along

the pond, a word
out there—the floor

hung between them—
with the dog in the reeds

continuing her dog-
like ways, and as if

balancing at the edge
before a fall, his father

had a name for it (then
the falling), he spoke

to him: a red flicker
to solid mass, arresting.

At the End of the Procession

And so the dull sound of soil
dropped against flat wood,

then the equally hard work,
our faces of decorum—

looking away from or towards—
to watch the hill fall away

behind the house. Remembrance
a depression, impact but still surface,

as we were told how it happened
and so was happening

(his explaining and not wanting to).
This is important to remember,

I remember thinking that.

Poppies

Do you remember how I wouldn't
    lift my eyes? That was this side
of the wall, away from the gallows
    and mass grave, yet right next to
the movie house and the drained
    children's swimming pool.
The thought of their laughter,
    of real water, was the cruel
gas I conjectured, filling Terezín
    until at night it choked

a child's sleep—not here,
    but on that side of the wall.
The sound of so much water
    had formed for a girl a sanctuary
to escape to in her painting
    (I saw it recently in a museum),
a desert oasis with palm trees,
    lions and the impossible giraffe.
A half-century after the camp closed,
    impossible glass flowers marked
the open gates, a cough caught

  in the throat.

The morning I left, on the long ride
    to the airport, short-cutting
through the outskirts of Prague
    along the taxi drivers' secret

route—a scenario for kidnapping
  and ransom: backcountry, dark
roads and an impossible language barrier.
  This is where I imagined tragedy
occurring to people like me,

like you. Except in our room,
  it was enough to a have a backdrop
of one vase stained to look
  antique and permanent
petals beneath the bare-bulb-
  white: a stage for pain's disclosure.

It wasn't our country,

        but it was
good to hear English, like the night
  we came upon the reading.
It almost redeemed me then
  to look at a flowerbox
above the alley, with its four or five
  red fists, representing flowers.
The darker it became, the closer
  I felt to being outside the walls
of the courtyard, where we were
  gathered. What murder in the Balkans
was being lamented by the raspy

Californian woman—her skin
soured from cigarettes and sun—
when she sang, *And gladioli*
are only fifteen crowns? What dream-
dark milk in the red flower's name?

The Dubliner

St. Paul, Minnesota

We'd drink there most weeknights, a bar
for sons and daughters of sons and daughters
of the Irish, who'd helped build the railroad

and wealth for Col. Crooks, but mostly
college kids there for live music, anthems
we understood about as much as annihilation,

the empty shot glasses' teetering pyramid,
so we cheered in hope for a nation
once again, cursing the goddamn yoke

of the Queen. Although, only one of my friends
ever went to Ireland, and he'd found no family
left there. His grandfather made a killing

trapping pigeons in Chicago before getting
on the wrong side of the wrong people
and moving to Minnesota. But for us

it was a different country, on the verge
of a new century, and we were drinking off the fat
of student loans, listening to a friend's band

play cover songs on Wednesdays, and when
Mike sang, "I want to fuck you like an animal,"
that whole compressed, postindustrial rage-turned-

folksong already seemed nostalgic, almost sweet,
like the thick marker scrawl, "Dow Jones
Keep On Rising," I'd seen graffitied

on the bathroom wall, in 1999; the bubble
lofting even us self-proclaimed poor
in smoke-filled circles above the scene.

Houses

In descent, a dark line where massy clouds start
    tightly formed across

buildings—*that coming out of*—a day edged
    with shadows, then without.

Enter the city at the level of gasoline, bars,
    billboards to compensate

injury. I find a shape for it, composed, troubling:
    I rhyme route with root.

—~—

I had a city. Where the street ends, the hill
    slopes, first vein

of yellow stone—where weeds thicken beneath
    trees, the trees

start, unplanned, unrowed—a shelf of yellow
    stone cuts, descending

to the banks. To stand there meant movement,
    an unreflecting substance.

—~—

A boulevard, a pattern, yards thick with trees.
        And if you should take comfort

in that? To come upon as in a wood, or turning
        flame, fumes churning

gears, motion into contagion. Enter here means
        descent. What fell into

would carry the imprint. *Would be self.* As in a house,
        as in I lived here once.

Up is good. There is a route to chart, sides to take
        in the giving and gaining ground

in the argument. *Here are many rooms.*
        Attic game, basement brawling—

What are you looking for? A passage way, a conduit,
        some hinge-like mechanism—

Which window was yours? The gray unreflecting
        substance of rivers, of lakes.

But a depth to it, a knowing that, inaccessible,
    waited there to answer back.

Where the trees began again, where the lit interiors
    of houses first showed

through leaves, I had another city.
                                        Leave the yard,

    let the gate grate shut.

Surfing for Caravaggio's *Conversion of Paul*

Enter keywords: Caravaggio, painter,
Santa Maria del Popolo. How many
people are contemplating paintings
at this moment? How many whips
and nipples? I had been reading a poem
about a poem about a Caravaggio,
in other words, a bar brawl—*beautiful*
horror as de Sade once called him—
but I don't get it, not having seen *it*.
While the computer emits an aura,
I guess, I don't have to go to Italy
to stand in line for a conversion,
or to be, as the poet says, *still falling.*
If a hundred people simultaneously
hold this painting in their minds,
will it gain a collective dullness,
a tarry film like too much smoke?
Are brushstrokes authentic, or the light?
Or the *salvation* (which doesn't share
a root with "salivate" or "salve"),
something saintly? No, he's still
only Saul. But Caravaggio painted
another version, and in this frame here,
nowhere near Santa Maria del Popolo,
it's over, and the new convert weeps—
out of shame? because his shirt's torn
open exposing his loose breasts?—
or he isn't weeping at all behind his hands.
If I were closer, I wouldn't understand

more about why he covers his eyes,
because with a *click* it's a throttled Isaac
staring out, ignoring both knife and canvas.

Notes

"*Novecento.*" The title and poem make reference to an installation by Maurizio Cattelan, which appeared in the 1998 exhibit, *Unfinished History*, at the Walker Art Center, Minneapolis.

"Conservatory." Frank Gehry's *Standing Glass Fish* can be found in the conservatory of the Minneapolis Sculpture Garden.

"Gorgias in Love." Gorgias (483-375 B.C.E), Sicilian philosopher, orator, and rhetorician. The poem makes reference to his lost text, *On the Nonexistent, or On Nature*, and roughly follows its three-part argument that 1) nothing exists, 2) even if existence exists, it cannot be known, and 3) even if it could be known, it cannot be communicated. The movie is Jean-Pierre Limosin's *Novo.*

"Noise Like Wings." The title and italicized phrases are taken from Samuel Beckett's *Waiting for Godot*. The poem is dedicated to Rick Barot.

"Event Horizon." The italicized words and phrase are taken from Keats's 13 March 1818 letter to Benjamin Bailey.

"The Physician at Wentworth Place." The italicized words and phrase are taken from Charles Brown's account of Keats's response to his severe hemorrhage of February 1820.

"Redwing Blackbird" and "At the End of the Procession." Dedicated to David Schlesinger and to the memory of Robert Schlesinger.

"Surfing for Caravaggio's *Conversion of Paul.*" The poem makes reference to and quotes a phrase from Stanley Plumly's "Comment on Thom Gunn's 'In Santa Maria Del Popolo' Concerning Caravaggio's *The Conversion of St. Paul.*" This poem is dedicated to him.

ACKNOWLEDGMENTS

Grateful acknowledgement is made to the editors of the following journals in which poems from this collection have previously appeared in these and other versions:

American Literary Review; Forklift, Ohio; Gulf Coast;
The Kenyon Review; Luna Magazine; Lyric; Marginalia;
New England Review; Pebble Lake Review; Virginia Quarterly Review.

"*Messiah*" was reprinted online at *Poetry Daily.*

For their guidance and friendship, which helped shape this book, I would like to thank Elizabeth Arnold, Rick Barot, Michael Collier, Mark Doty, Patricia Hampl, Brian Nicolet, Stanley Plumly, Claudia Rankine, Martha Rhodes, and Joshua Weiner. I'd also like to thank the Bread Loaf Writers' Conference and the Inprint organization for their support. The gratitude I owe to my brother, Matthew, is immeasurable.

Paul Otremba's poems and criticism have appeared in such places as *The Kenyon Review, New England Review, Poetry Daily, Tikkun, Virginia Quarterly Review,* and *American Poets in the 21st Century: The New Poetics.* He has won an Academy of American Poets prize, a Barthelme Memorial Fellowship, scholarships to the Bread Loaf Writers' Conference, and a Krakow Poetry Seminar Fellowship. He received his MFA from the University of Maryland, and he is completing his PhD at the University of Houston.